Make Your Own

MOBILES

By T. M. SCHEGGER

STERLING
PUBLISHING CO., INC.
NEW YORK

Oak Tree Press Co., Ltd.
London & Sydney

STERLING CRAFTS BOOKS

Cardboard Crafting
Carpentry for Children
Complete Crayon Book
Creating from Scrap
Creative Claywork
Creative Enamelling & Jewelry- Making
Creative Leathercraft
Creative Paper Crafts in Color
Etching (and Other Intaglio Techniques)

How to Make Things Out of Pap
Make Your Own Mobil
Making Mosai
Original Creations with Papier Mâch
Papier Mâché—and How to Use
Prints—from Linoblocks and Woodcu
Sculpture for Beginne
Stained Glass Craftin
Tin-Can Craftin

Weaving as a Hobby

Family Book of Crafts
Practical Encyclopedia of Crafts

Photograph on page 5 by courtesy of The Port of New York Authority.

Translated by Paul Kuttner; adapted by Robert F. Scott

Eleventh Printing, 1973
Copyright © 1965 by Sterling Publishing Co., Inc.
419 Park Avenue South, New York, N.Y. 10016
British edition published by Oak Tree Press Co., Ltd., Nassau, Bahamas
Distributed in Australia and New Zealand by Oak Tree Press Co., Ltd.,
P.O. Box 34, Brickfield Hill, Sydney 2000, N.S.W.
Distributed in the United Kingdom and elsewhere in the British Commonwealth
by Ward Lock Ltd., 116 Baker Street, London W 1
Original edition published in 1963 in German
under the title "Das Mobile-Bastelbuch" by the Don Bosco Verlag, Munich
Manufactured in the United States of America
All rights reserved
Library of Congress Catalog Card No.: 64-24683
ISBN 0- 8069–5066–8   UK 7061 2029 9
5067–6

1. Mobiles (Sculpture)
I. Title

Contents

This mobile by Alexander Calder is the largest in the world.   It
hangs in the International Arrivals Building, John F. Kennedy Air-
port, New York City.

Alexander Calder

This book is respectfully dedicated to Alexander Calder

Introduction

How did mobiles originate? Do they spring from someone's watching branches stirring in the breeze and leaves in movement, silhouetted against the transparent backdrop of twilight? Do they take their inspiration from the flapping arms of primitive windmills, the first of the machines devised by man? Or do they perhaps have a kinship with the beaded doorways and the tinkling wind-blown chimes of the East?

Although mobiles may have such deep-rooted origins, their recorded history is curiously brief. For all practical purposes, they have constituted a separate art form for little more than thirty years. The first mobile constructed in the style now familiar to us was conceived by Alexander Calder, an American artist, in about 1931, and was first exhibited in Paris in 1932.

Because Calder, the "father of mobiles," had been a sculptor of sorts (his father and grandfather were both famous sculptors) and because of the mobile's sometimes sculptural qualities, it is customary to see in mobiles a link with traditional sculpture and to call them "mobile sculptures." However, they could just as easily be defined as "mobile three-dimensional paintings" because of their qualities of color and their often flattened shapes.

The important thing about mobiles is not whether they are a form of sculpture or painting but that they move (the word "mobile" meaning "movable"). Not only do they move, but mobiles give pleasure in their action and in their ever-changing appearance. Also, they can be created and enjoyed by anyone, regardless of age, artistic training or sophistication. In these qualities lies their unique charm and appeal.

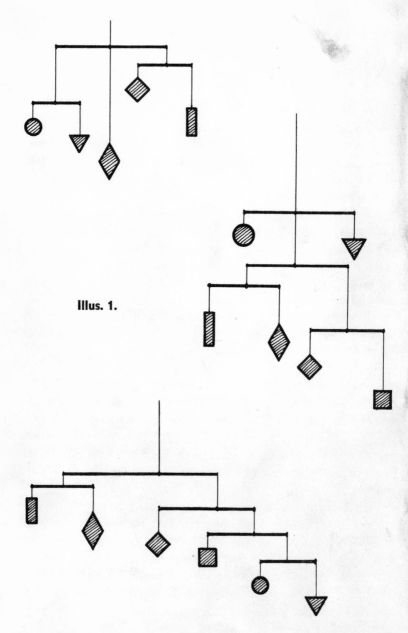

Illus. 1.

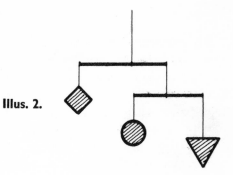

Illus. 2.

Fun with Composition and Balance

A mobile consists of various objects created, adapted or selected by the maker of the mobile and arranged and balanced on one or more wire arms so that they are free to move in space, either with respect to or independent of one another.

This, in its essentials, is a definition of a mobile. Note that the objects making up the mobile may be created, adapted or *selected* by the maker of the mobile. Thus, a coin collector for his amusement, or a coin dealer for use as a display, could create a mobile merely by selecting certain coins and suspending them by threads from wire arms. This would not be a mobile such as you would see in an art museum, but it would still be a mobile by any definition.

Of course, a mobile composed of things you have created will always be more personally satisfying than a mobile made from things that you have selected. For example, try making the figures described on the next few pages and see for yourself just how easy and how much fun *making* the component parts of a mobile can be.

FLAT FISH

Anyone who can use a pair of scissors can make a whole school of these flat fish in a few minutes' time. Cut a series of simple, angular forms as shown in Illustration 3. They don't have to be all of the same size or shape—in fact, they will look better when assembled in a mobile if they display a wide variety of sizes and shapes. Use cardboard, heavy metal foil or patterned gift-wrapping paper. For an unusual effect, cover the cardboard "fish" with paper-thin adhesive-backed wood veneers, alternating the grain direction from fish to fish. Or paint the cardboard shapes in gay colors.

For something different, try this unusual material: Paste cut-open plastic straws on a piece of cardboard and cut out fish with a rugged, corduroy-textured surface.

When your fish are completed, punch the single hole for the eye using a small hand punch.

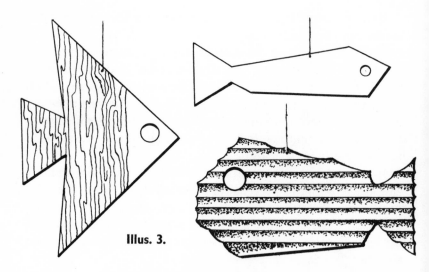

Illus. 3.

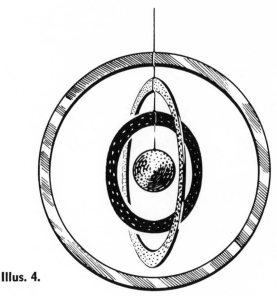

Illus. 4.

Here is a mobile whose parts can move in several directions at the same time.

Cut three or four cardboard rings in diminishing sizes from different pieces of colored cardboard. Each ring should be about $\frac{1}{2}''$ in width, and the largest can be up to $12''$ in diameter. When you cut your series of rings, be sure they are at least an inch or two apart in diameter. If you have rings of $6''$, $9''$ and $12''$, for example, you will find that they swing smoothly (Illustration 4).

In the middle hang a table-tennis ball that you have painted in a complementary or contrasting color.

Connect the rings by looping thread around them. Knot the end of the thread and insert it in the table-tennis ball in a hole you have made using a sharp tack. A dab of model cement will keep the knot from pulling out.

Illus. 5.

DANCERS

Next, try something different. Trace the parts of the dancing figures on heavy glazed paper and cut them out. Note that the head, arms and lower body are separate. Join the parts using fine thread through the balance points shown in Illustration 5. Make your dancing figures more colorful by using a different colored paper for each segment.

Of course you are not limited to the four figures shown in the illustration. Cut out your own figures, change their poses or change their costumes.

FLAT GEOMETRICAL SHAPES

In your first experiments at making a mobile, you have probably discovered that there are many different effects that can be achieved by changing shapes ever so slightly or by the addition of a complementary or clashing color. Now is the time to experiment in earnest with this part of mobile making. For example, create squares, triangles, diamond-shaped lozenges, rectangles, circles, ovals and free-form shapes from colored cardboard. Experiment with the effect of introducing variety in color as well as in shape into a geometrical mobile. Note the effect of mixing the angular straight-sided figures with the curved shapes. There's more to making mobiles than just hanging objects from wires, isn't there? And there's fun in discovering the effects of changes in composition and balance.

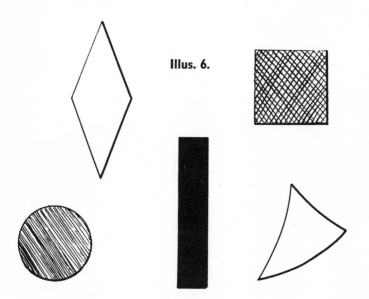

Illus. 6.

THREE-DIMENSIONAL GEOMETRICAL SHAPES

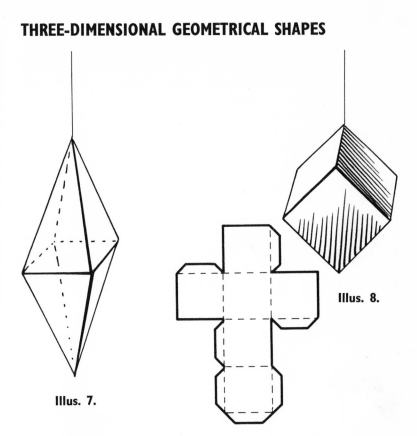

Illus. 7.

Illus. 8.

Make cubes, pyramids, cones, cylinders and cylinder-cone combinations, as shown in Illustrations 7 to 10. These can be of glazed or unglazed heavy colored paper or light-weight cardboard. Fold each shape along the fold lines indicated by the dashed lines.

Now fold and glue the protruding glue tabs inside the figures. A mobile made with geometrical shapes makes an exciting decoration in a classroom or for the room of someone who has just discovered the world of mathematics for the first time.

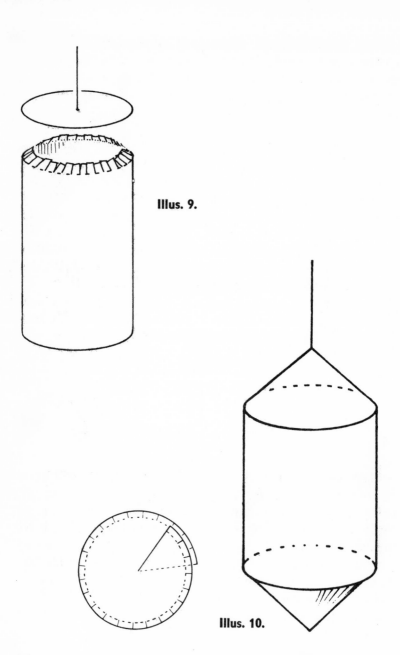

Illus. 9.

Illus. 10.

Once having created, adapted or selected the objects for inclusion in a mobile, your only problem will be the arrangement or placement of the particular objects. The arranging of these objects in space—indeed the incorporation of the very space itself into the mobile—requires a certain knowledge of composition; the particular placement of these objects on the arms of the mobile and their relationship to the structure of the mobile as a whole will be an exercise in balance.

You can acquire skill in composition and balance by experimentation. For example, place an identical coin at each end of a foot-long ruler. The balance point, as you know without even attempting the experiment, will be exactly midway between each end. The same is true for a mobile: The balance point for two equal objects will be at the exact middle of the supporting arm. (See Illustration 11.)

Now place two identical coins at one end of the ruler and only one coin at the other end. The balance point, as you undoubtedly have guessed, has now shifted toward the two

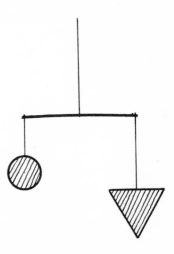

Illus. 11.

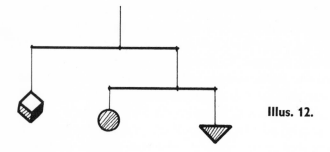

Illus. 12.

coins, so that you need to add weight to the ruler on the opposite (and longer) side to counterbalance the two coins. But just how far has the exact point of balance been moved? You can only find out by trial and error.

Of course, the parts of a mobile do not always have to be in perfect balance. If you fasten two coins at one end of your ruler and one at the other end and balance the ruler at about 6 inches, you will notice that the ruler will incline itself at an angle and eventually come to rest and hold the inclined position. We now say that this whole system of coins and ruler is in equilibrium, even though it is not horizontally and symmetrically balanced.

So it is with a mobile, too. Two objects on one arm of a mobile may be asymmetrically balanced in equilibrium by a single object if you vary their position slightly or alter the position of the balance point. To achieve perfect balance, if, for example, you were using a cardboard cut-out mobile, you could make the single side heavier by using a larger piece of cardboard or by using two smaller pieces of cardboard glued together (double-thickness), thus equalling in weight the two pieces on the opposite side. (See Illustration 12.) Or you could balance two cardboard objects with one of a heavier material, such as tin.

If even balance is *not* your goal in the design and construction of the arms of your mobile, you will have more opportunities to experiment artistically with variations in shapes, sizes and placements. The important rule to remember about mobiles is that there are no rules. You are not limited in any way in the making of a mobile—there are no conventions regarding placement, suspension, color, shape, texture, thickness or the nature of the materials that you use. You can create a mobile from cardboard, metal, glass, wood, stone or any other material. You can use eggs, fruit, nuts, wood chips, driftwood or shavings, Christmas tree ornaments, table tennis balls, gift wrapping materials, metal foil—even arsenic and old lace. The shapes you select can be representational and recognizable or abstract and random free-forms. They can range from the sublime to the ridiculous.

An important element in composition and balance is color. For example, try this experiment: Make a two-part mobile (like the one shown in Illustration 13), from grey cardboard and suspend it from a length of wire, using heavy sewing

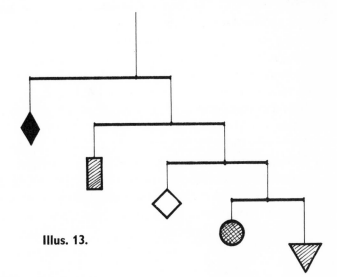

Illus. 13.

thread. Notice the effect achieved as it slowly moves. Using poster color or nail polish, paint one side of one piece a bright red and blacken the other side with crayon. Now notice how the whole effect of the mobile is changed as the flashes of color on one side are offset by the blackness of the other side. You can experiment further by increasing the number of parts of your mobile and achieving variety with occasional flashes of added color.

Start with the primary colors (red, yellow and blue) plus white, black and grey in your experiments in balance and composition. Later include the secondary colors (green, orange and purple) to give yourself a wider color range. See the back cover of this book for an application of the principle of balance in color.

When you come to create your own mobiles, remember that the space in which a mobile hangs and moves is an important part of its composition and balance. Placement in space is as important as the objects used to make the mobile, or their color, shape, and arrangement. In other words, space— the absence of color or form—must be taken into consideration in the planning of a mobile. How to use space properly in placing your mobile is easily learned.

For example, there are nine planets in the solar system, some with moons revolving around them. (Earth has one, Mars two, Neptune two, Uranus five, Saturn nine and Jupiter twelve.) Imagine that you have constructed a mobile of the sun, the planets and their moons so that they all revolve as they do in the solar system. Such a "mobile" might interest an astronomer, but it soon would become boring to watch. Consider the same mobile constructed so that all of the parts are capable of random movement. How much more interesting this mobile would be!

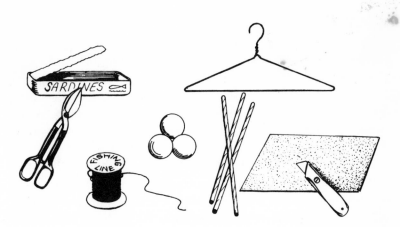

Materials For Mobiles

In order to make the rest of the mobiles in this book, you will need certain materials to work with. The range is not great, nor are the materials fixed as to type. You should try always to improvise: If you have no artists' illustration board, use shirt cardboard. If you need a piece of tin, try snipping it from a ham tin (or other large tin-can with a flat surface). If you need a piece of wire and have none handy, a thin wire coat hanger might be the answer. In mobiles, the important thing to remember is that improvisation should be your first resort, rather than the last.

CARDBOARD

You will need two different thicknesses of cardboard. These can be artists' illustration board or poster board. For your larger mobiles, get medium-weight and heavy-weight cardboard and avoid too-thin or too-light thicknesses, which are liable to warp. Oak-tag, a flexible, easily cut, hard finished, glazed cardboard, is ideal for making many of the projects in this book that call for the bending and folding of the cardboard.

PAPER

Paper has the advantage that it is light, easily cut, and easily bent or worked. If fairly stiff and fresh, it will assume and hold given shapes. Its flexibility makes it ideal for applications where wind movement will be the motive power behind the mobile.

SHEET METAL

Sheet tin (actually a galvanized and thinly rolled sheet of iron) can be obtained from a tinsmith's or roofer's supply house. For most purposes, a thickness of .006 inch (sometimes called "tagger's tin") and .012 inch will be the most useful in mobiles. Tin should be cut with tin snips or tinsmith's shears.

PLASTIC

Sheets of clear or colored plastic can be used in mobiles. An advantage is that they can be easily cut and cemented together and—if colored—that they do not need to be painted.

GLASS

Although not so easily worked as plastic, metal or cardboard, glass in sheets or pieces is a popular material with mobile makers. Its wide range of colors and its transparent, translucent or iridescent qualities account for its popularity. It must be cut with a glass cutter.

MISCELLANEOUS MATERIALS

Diversified materials include nuts and fruit, table-tennis balls, driftwood bits, wood shavings, and drinking straws, both natural and plastic tubing types—in fact anything that you may want to use. The only limitations will be those imposed by the physical ability of the supporting materials to hold up the materials you select, adapt or create.

PAINTS

Get an assortment of poster (tempera) colors from your art supply dealers for painting your mobiles—unless you intend to hang them out of doors or to expose them to extreme conditions. If your mobile will be subject to the deteriorating effects of moisture, it is better to use oil paints. These can be bought in tubes or small-sized tin-cans. However, remember that outdoor mobiles tend to deteriorate unless the paint is renewed frequently.

THREAD

Nylon thread or nylon fishing line are best for suspending mobile parts, but heavy sewing thread may be substituted if necessary.

WIRE

Galvanized iron wire, most frequently used as fencing, is the most easily obtainable wire and can be bought at most hardware suppliers'. Wire thicknesses are measured and described in gauges. The most useful gauges for the maker of mobiles will be Nos. 18, 16, 14 and 12. (The wire gets thicker as the gauge number decreases.)

GLUE

Any of the modern polyvinyl resin glues can be used in making mobiles, particularly if the joint will be subject to stress. For most purposes in making mobiles, however, ordinary acetone-base household cement in tubes will be adequate. The latter has the advantage of quick drying time. It is especially useful for attaching supporting threads to the wire arms once the balance point has been determined.

TIPS ON TOOLS

If the materials with which you will make your mobiles are only paper and cardboard, you will need only a pair of scissors or a sharp knife and a pair of pliers. Although you will be able to cut cardboard with your scissors, you will probably find that a sharp knife, such as a picture framer's mat knife or a patented knife with a replaceable blade, will do a neater job and will make more intricate cuts.

Your pliers should be the long-nosed type, with jaws about 4 inches long. Get the kind with side cutters in the jaws. You will use the pliers to cut wires and to bend loops in the wires with which your mobiles will be hung (Illustration 14).

If you elect to work with sheet tin, then compound leverage shears or tin snips (preferably with serrated edges) are a requisite. Cutting tin is not difficult, as you will discover once you try it. But exercise reasonable care in handling the tin to see that you do not cut yourself. (The serrated edges prevent this.)

The cutting of glass is not difficult either, but be particularly careful not to cut yourself when handling glass. A simple glass cutter's wheel cuts quickly and easily once you learn the technique.

Always cut glass on a firm, flat surface. If you are cutting along a straight line, use a steel straightedge to guide the cutting wheel. Bear down firmly and draw the wheel once across the glass. A tap at the scored line with the other end of the cutting tool will often be enough to start the glass breaking along the scored line. If the glass does not break easily, try to bend the two sides of the glass slightly, keeping the scored line away from you. The glass should give easily.

Illus. 14.

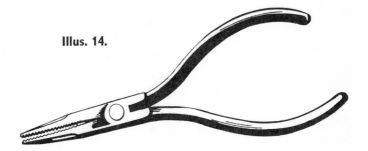

Illus. 15.

Hanging Your Mobiles

Mobiles can only be appreciated if they are displayed. The best way to display an indoor mobile is to suspend it from the ceiling or from a light fixture affixed to the ceiling.

Unfortunately, even the lightest of the mobiles in this book, when complete with wire arms, will be too heavy for suspensions using transparent plastic tape to affix them to the ceiling.

You have several alternatives among fastening techniques: Most nails will pull right out of the ceiling unless corrugated or ribbed roofing or flooring nails are used.

Lead, fibre, or plastic plugs, sold under various trade-marked names can be purchased. These are inserted into holes drilled in the ceiling. (Be sure the hole is only as deep as the plug is long.) When a screw is screwed into the plug, it expands to grip the plaster sides of the hole.

The most satisfactory and long-lasting technique is to use one of several flange-type fastening devices marketed under several names. To mount these, drill a hole in the ceiling of the same diameter as the device and insert it. A bolt, which is part of the assembly, is then screwed in. This draws the back of the device forward and causes the flange-like wings of the device to expand. Because these "wings" expand behind the plaster ceiling, there is no chance for the device to be pulled out. You simply back off the bolt slightly and a thread or wire can be attached to the bolt head.

Outdoor mobiles, of course, can be suspended from posts, poles or tree branches.

Now On To Making Mobiles

There are no hard and fast rules for the planning and making of mobiles, for there cannot be rules governing an art form which is so much an expression of the artistic taste and individuality of the maker.

Generally speaking, mobiles are made "from the bottom up." That is to say, you will start by assembling the lower-most arm or arms and add others above them. You can usually change a mobile consisting of, say, three parts to one of five, ten, or any greater number, simply by adding additional parts at the top. This is not to say that you cannot *design* a mobile and—having its design fixed in mind or on paper—proceed to construct your mobile from the top down. But in your early, experimental mobiles you will certainly want to start at the lower level and work upwards, adding the higher levels as you proceed.

Cardboard mobile parts can be attached to wires or thread through punched holes and by looping or tying the wires and threads. Or, they may be joined with glue. Metal mobile pieces can be soldered to wire arms; if suspended from them, the tin pieces can be punched to receive threads or fine wires or the loops of the wire arms.

Use your long-nosed pliers to form loops in the wire arms. If you will examine the pliers, you will see that the jaws are round at the tip and gradually take an oval shape farther from the tip. To make a round loop, grasp the end of the wire in the jaws of the pliers near the tip and form a loop with a quick twisting motion of your wrist. (See Illustration 16.) If you want an oval loop rather than a round loop, simply grasp the wire between the jaws farther from the tip.

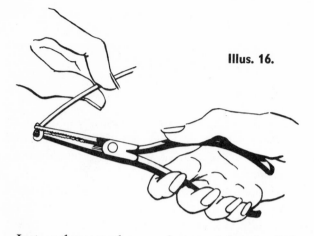

Illus. 16.

Just as there can be no rules governing the design of mobiles, there can be few fixed dimensions for objects or designated lengths of support arms, lengths of suspension threads, etc. Similarly, *you*, the maker of *your* mobile, will have to decide whether you wish your assemblages to hang in symmetrical horizontal balance or to be balanced in asymmetrical equilibrium.

Whether your wire support arms will be straight or will curve in gentle arcs is also something which you will have to decide. In fact, the supreme satisfaction to the maker of mobiles (unless, of course, he merely copies an existing mobile) lies in the fact that the mobile he creates is something new and original and unlike anything else.

For example, you can make a Christmas tree mobile with wire arms painted green, and with Christmas tree ornaments and decorations suspended from them. But no two such mobile trees will be alike. Just as no two decorated Christmas trees are ever exactly alike, so the ornaments you select, the lengths to which you cut the wire arms, and the total effect that you achieve will be the unique result of your own efforts. If it can be said of any art form, it can be said that making mobiles is a true expression of the individual and his taste.

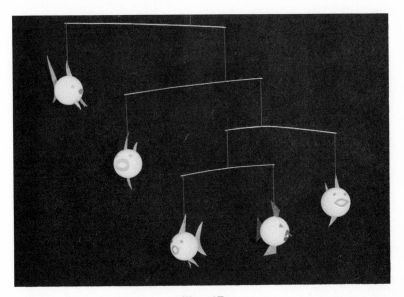

Illus. 17.

Don't discard table-tennis balls that have lost their bounce—convert them into these globular ball fish.

Carefully make small incisions into a table-tennis ball with a sharp knife and insert into the slits various fin designs cut from colored cardboard.

Glue flat, colored paper eyes and mouths on the ball bodies after cutting them from glazed paper.

You can also make the eyes and mouth in three-dimensional fashion from several layers of colored paper or a piece of colored paper glued on medium-weight cardboard. (See the second fish from the right in Illustration 17.)

Fix the suspension thread to the top of the dorsal (back) fin.

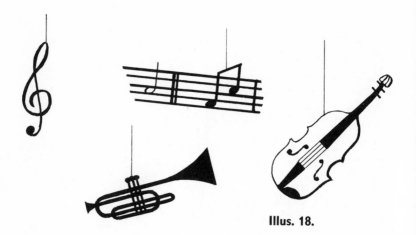

Illus. 18.

MUSICAL MOTIF MOBILES

Any music student would be delighted with a mobile with a musical motif. Or make such a mobile as a class project for your school's music room.

On heavy black paper or cardboard trace the outline of a musical clef and musical notes. Make a musical staff from plastic straws as shown in Illustration 18. Paint these black for a more realistic look.

Paste the clef and the notes on the staff. For a more ambitious musical motif mobile, cut out silhouettes in heavy black paper of various musical instruments—violin, tuba, clarinet, piano. Suspend these as part of your mobile.

Music lovers will also appreciate receiving the gift of a mobile made up of easily recognized snatches of music— the opening bars of Beethoven's Fifth Symphony or some other immediately recognizable theme. Or make a mobile from the notes of their favorite tune.

In the autumn when walnuts are plentiful, open some of them carefully so as to keep both halves of each walnut in an undamaged condition. (Although you can use *any* two halves of walnut shells, you will find that both halves of the same shell will give a better fit and a better final appearance to your walnut fish.)

From colored paper, cut out fins and tails. These can be of various shapes: half-moon, jagged-edged, scalloped-edged, or feathery. (Even fluffy feathers can be used for fins and tail.) For more colorful fish, spray or paint the empty walnut halves with bright quick-drying colors.

Now glue the two halves of each shell together, making sure that the fins and tail remain where you have placed them while the two halves were drying.

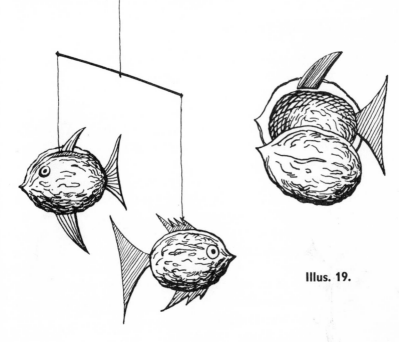

Illus. 19.

TRANSPARENT FISH

Fish like these have an Oriental quality about them. Their transparency gives them a special airy effect.

Illus. 20.

Bend a piece of thin wire 10″ long into the simple shape shown in Illustration 20. Tie a short length of thread or very fine wire at the point where the wire crosses itself to hold the joint together.

Now lightly coat one side of the wire with glue. Lay the wire fish on a piece of tightly stretched tracing paper or rice paper. When the glue has dried, cut around the fish, leaving a margin of about ⅛″ extra. Make a few vertical snips into this edge to divide it into segments and glue this around the back of the wire. Cut the edge of the fish's tail in a series of scalloped notches to give a scaly effect. Paste a small round circle of colored paper on the fish to serve as an eye.

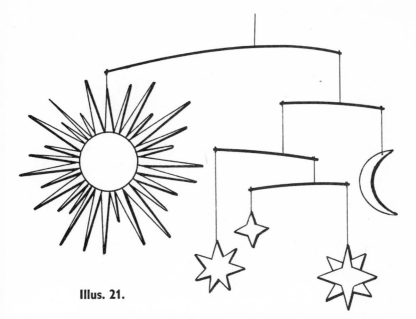

Illus. 21.

CELESTIAL BODIES

No matter how little you may know of astronomy, you can create your own model of the universe in a mobile.

Sketch the shape of a many-rayed sun, four-, five- and seven-pointed stars, a quarter moon, and other "celestial bodies." (If you feel ambitious, you can add Saturn and its rings, the red planet, Mars, and perhaps a space rocket or two.)

Transfer your sketches on to colored paper or metal foil. Make the sun bright gold, the stars silver, and the moon yellow.

FRUIT MOBILES

Illus. 22.

Sketch on cardboard or heavy paper the outlines of various fruits—oranges, apples, lemons, bananas, pears. (Be sure to leave stems on the apples and pears—they will make the attachment of the fruit easier.)

Color the fruit on each side. Suspend the fruit from lightweight wire hanger arms using very fine thread. The fruit will seem to be floating through the air.

Another way of getting fruit for your fruit mobiles is to cut pictures of fruit from magazines or newspapers. Color these in the pages of the magazine or newspaper (if they are not already colored) before you cut them out and you will find that the coloring is much easier.

There is nothing more amusing to watch than a mobile of cork birds, darting and dancing about.

The body of each bird is a colored or undyed cork (Illustration 23). Cut the beak from glazed paper. A table-tennis ball will do nicely for the bird's head. Impale both the beak and the head of the bird on a long pin and press its pointed end into the cork until the head meets the body.

Next, stick some dyed feathers to simulate wings and tail into the cork. Drill holes for these beforehand with a thick needle and fasten the feathers in the holes with drops of glue.

Fasten the suspension thread at the balance point by means of a small tack or pin stuck into the cork body of the bird.

Illus. 23.

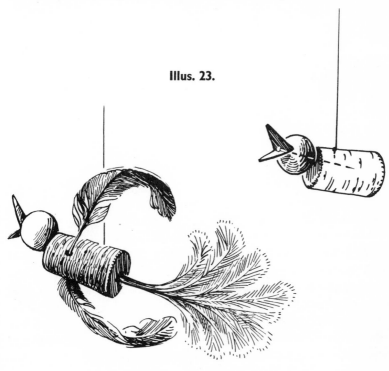

FLAT SAILBOATS

Sailboats will make a charming mobile, especially if they are of varying sizes, types and colors.

Cut the hull of each boat from dark cardboard; this will make a nice contrast with the white of the sails. (See Illustration 24.) You may vary the shape of the hulls from boat to boat—making sloops, schooners, three-masted barks, etc.

Next cut out triangular sails, each one separately. Dab a drop of glue on the lower corner of the smaller sail and fix it to the boat's other side. Glue the second sail on to the opposite side of the boat so that the rear part of the front sail overlaps the front of the second sail. (Do the same for any additional sails if you equip any of your sailboats with more than two sails.)

Illus. 24.

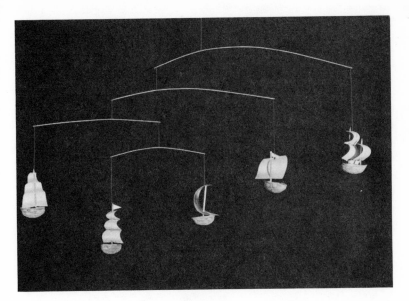

Illus. 25.

NUTSHELL SAILBOATS

When you have enjoyed nutmeats, don't discard the shells. Save them for use in your next mobile.

Fill one half of an empty nutshell (walnut shells are the best for this purpose) with modelling clay. Insert a toothpick or long thin stick into this clay, and fasten a galleon-type sail to it by impaling it on the mast. (Pricking the two holes beforehand with a sharp knife will help to get them started.) Examine the boats in Illustration 25 for hints on the various kinds of sails that you can hoist on your nutshell sailboats.

BEECHNUT BIRDS

When autumn comes, collect some of the nuts that beech trees shed. Do not detach the stem which looks like a long, pointed bird's beak. Split each beechnut husk at the other end and hollow it out somewhat. Now stick the wings and the tail feathers into this space.

To make your birds as lifelike as possible, paint the beak yellow or bright red and apply two dots of blue or green paint to the head for eyes. (See Illustration 26.) Beechnut birds make an unusually attractive mobile.

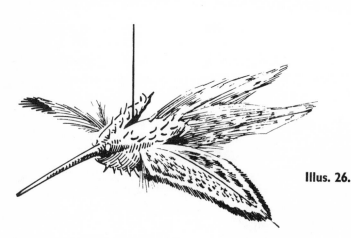

Illus. 26.

Illus. 27.

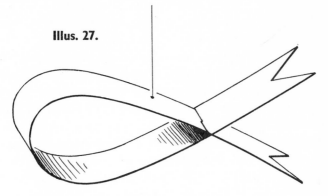

These paper fish are so simple to make that you can transform any spot into a make-believe "underwater" locale with a few snips of your scissors.

Cut a piece of heavy paper or light-weight flexible cardboard into strips 1″ (one inch) wide and 10″ long. Cut a slit 1½″ from each end, halfway through the strip from opposite sides. (These slits will "lock" the fish in position when it is assembled). Notch the tail pieces as shown in Illustration 28 and assemble your fish.

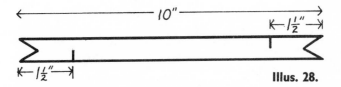

Illus. 28.

Connect the fish to the wire arms with nylon thread. The simplest way to do this is to make a small pinhole at the balance point of the fish as shown in illustrations. Make a knot or knots in the end of the thread and thread it upwards through the pinhole so that the knot holds against the cardboard. A dab of glue on the knot will make it more secure.

SPINY PAPER FISH

A spiny paper fish looks dangerous, but isn't. His "spines" will make him move merrily in the slightest breeze.

Make the strip for this fish a little longer—about 12" x 1", using the same flexible cardboard or paper as for the preceding fish. Cut the locking slits halfway through from each side, as in the preceding project. One slit is $1\frac{1}{2}$" from one end, the other slit is 4" from the opposite end. Also cut two sets of five $1\frac{1}{2}$"-wide slits as shown in Illustration 29. One set will lie between $2\frac{1}{2}$" and 4" from the short end, the other between $5\frac{1}{2}$" and 8".

Cut five strips of the same material, each measuring 3" x $\frac{1}{2}$". Fold them each in half and insert them in the slits already cut in the "body" of the fish. Lock the fish by sliding the two half slits together and join the tail with some transparent tape. Fold a mouth in the "head" as in the illustration, and your fish is ready to hang.

Make larger fish by doubling the dimensions or by halving them and adding them to the original measurements.

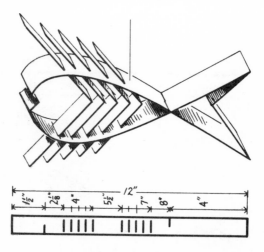

Illus. 29.

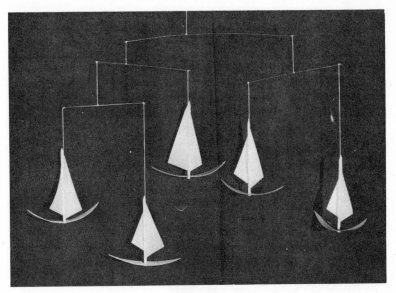

Illus. 30.

WOOD-CHIP SAILBOATS

Get your local carpenter or cabinet-maker to save you a bag of wood chips or long shavings that come from the planer. You can also use driftwood splinters for this project. Whatever you use should be dyed a bright color.

Make the hull of your boat by whittling the wood to a point at both ends. Next, carefully drill a small hole in the middle of the wood. Now take a piece of white thin cardboard or white stiff paper and cut it into the shape of a sail. Glue a small dowel (or toothpick) down the middle of the sail so that it protrudes $\frac{1}{2}''$ below the bottom edge. Next, place the mast and sail into the hole you have prepared and wedge it tight.

Your mobile will look particularly attractive if your fleet of boats have hulls and sails of contrasting colors.

BALLOONS

You can recapture the days of early aeronautics with a mobile full of dancing balloons. Tiny figures in the baskets will complete the picture.

Make the balloons from table-tennis balls. Clean smudged balls—and take off manufacturers' imprints—with fine emery paper. If you want a mobile of many colored balloons, paint the individual table tennis balls with poster colors. Let them dry.

Now brush the middle of two pieces of wool yarn 10″ long with glue (a distance of about 1″). Stretch these "cables" over the ball, crossing them at right angles. Let these dry.

Make a small basket out of light-weight cardboard (following Illustration 31) and cover it with a scrap of coarse cloth. Illustration 32 shows what your finished free balloons will look like.

Hang from the mid-point by puncturing the ball and stuffing your knotted thread through the hole. If you hang one balloon low over a table and others high, it will give the impression that the balloons are ascending.

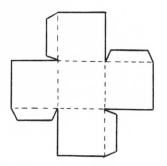

Illus. 31.

Illus. 32.

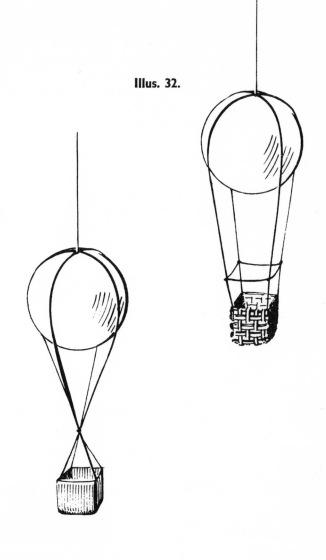

ROUND FISH

A mobile constructed with round fish will dance merrily for you. It will be especially effective if you make your round fish of different sizes; this gives the effect of distance.

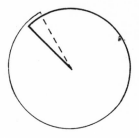

Illus. 33.

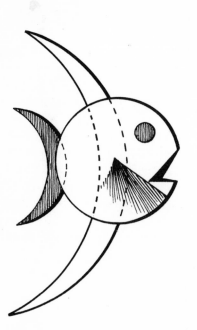

Illus. 34.

Illus. 35.

Make round fish by cutting two circular parts for each fish from glazed colored paper. Use coins or tin-cans of various sizes as guides for drawing your circles. Cut an incision in each part extending from the edge to the mid-point. Insert one circular segment into the other so that there is about ¼″ of overlap. Now glue the two segments together (Illustration 33).

Cut the fins from contrasting colored paper, making them moon-shaped, as shown in Illustration 34.

Cut a notch for the fish's mouth. Add circular patches of contrasting paper on each side for the eyes.

Illustration 35 shows a finished mobile made with round fish.

PAPER STRIP MOBILES

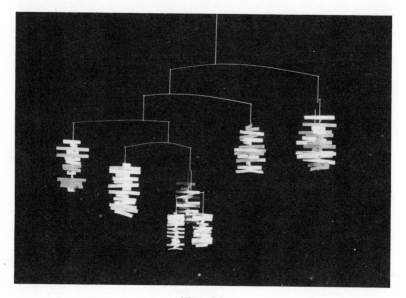

Illus. 36.

Long an art in the Orient, paper cutting and folding have now come west.

The mobiles in Illustration 36 are made of paper strips and are not difficult to create. First, sketch out the strips, as in the photograph, on heavy drawing paper or very light cardboard. Next mark the middle with a line through each of the strips.

Cut the strips apart. (If you wish, you can cut your strips from sheets of different colored papers, alternating them when you start the next step.) Now, using a sewing machine set for a big stitch (about $\frac{1}{4}''$) sew the separate strips together along the axial line you have drawn down the middle of the strips. If the stitches are too close together they will perforate the strips, so avoid this. Sew the strips so there is no separation between the strips either.

Knot the tail end of the sewing thread at the bottom and leave a long piece of thread at the top for suspending the paper strip mobile.

Many variations of this mobile are possible. (See Illustration 37.) Your paper strip mobiles can be square, rectangular, oval or round in shape. They can be made irregular by varying the length of the strips you use. Varying the type of paper used for the strips will also change the effect of such a mobile, particularly when it is blown by the wind.

You can hang round strips to balance rectangular strips, or make separate hangings.

WHIRLING BALLS

A mobile made of whirling balls makes an excellent decoration for a birthday party or other festive occasion.

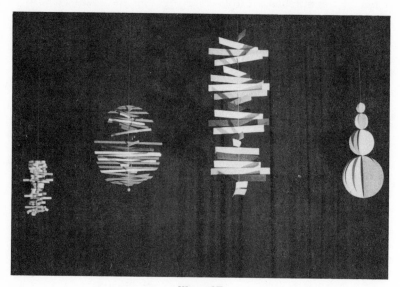

Illus. 37.

Cut three or four varicolored discs of equal size from heavy glazed paper or light-weight cardboard. Choose a different colored paper or cardboard for each disc.

Place these discs one on top of another and draw a line through the middle of the top disc. Next sew them together along this line with a sewing machine, using a wide ($\frac{1}{4}''$) stitch.

Fan the half-discs outwards in both directions and you will have a "ball" made up of fan-like segments. These will whirl merrily in the breeze if you incorporate several of different sizes into one mobile, as shown in Illustration 37.

You can turn out dozens of these intricate folded fish by having a group of people all fold the fish at the same time, following the directions as read by you.

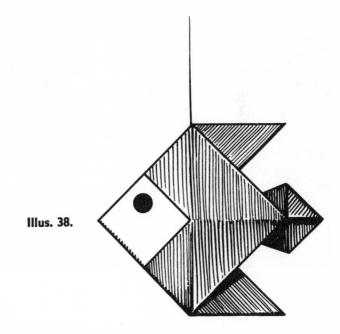

Illus. 38.

Cut a piece of glazed paper 8½" square. Fold it from corner to diagonally opposite corner into a triangle. Open it and fold it into a new triangle in the diagonally opposite direction. Open it again. It will look like Illustration 39. Next, fold the opened square of paper in half in each direction, bringing one side to the mid-point, then the other. Fold all four sides in this fashion.

Now fold the four corners of the paper square to the middle. A smaller square will result. Turn this so that the flaps are

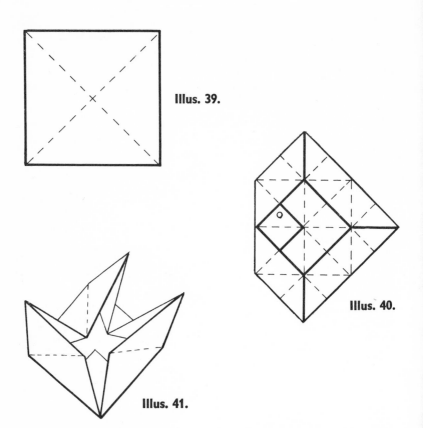

Illus. 39.

Illus. 40.

Illus. 41.

face down (without opening it). Fold the four corners of this smaller square to the middle again so that a still smaller square results.

Now unfold everything again all the way with the exception of the first corner that you folded toward the middle. Your paper will look like Illustration 40. Mark on the paper the square shown in Illustration 40. This will later delineate the fish's head and body. (The objective of all of this folding has been to get some guide lines and fold lines on the paper.) Pinch the sides of the three unfolded corners together so that they look like Illustration 41.

Next fold these pinched pleats down. (Illustration 42 shows what they look like from the other side.) The middle fold will become the tail fin; the other two folds are the dorsal (back) and pectoral (belly) fins. Fold the middle fold (tail fin) as shown in Illustration 43.

Make a second fish of the same size just like the first. The only difference is that the final tail fin fold on this second fish is made by folding the pleat in the opposite direction than before. If the tail fin on the first fish was folded toward the dorsal fin, fold the tail fin on the second fish toward the pectoral fin, and vice versa.

Paste the two halves of the fish together. The finished fish looks like Illustration 38.

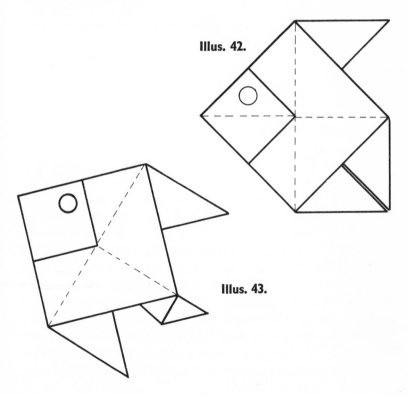

Illus. 42.

Illus. 43.

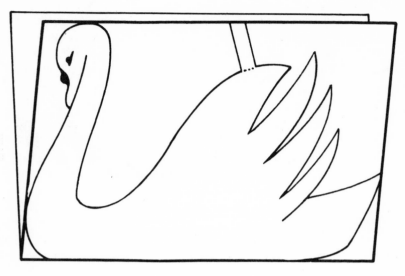

Illus. 44.

SWANS AND DUCKS

A mobile can capture the majesty of sailing waterfowl—in fact, there is something about the serene movement of the components of a mobile that makes it ideal for such representation.

Draw the basic outlines of these birds on folded drawing paper, following Illustrations 44 and 45. Cut out the shapes through both thicknesses, leaving the bottom part folded and the top open. Glue the features of the head and throat to their opposite counterparts, but spread the upper parts of the body apart, giving your bird rounded contours.

Now join and glue together the two narrow tabs which are attached to the bodies and which serve to keep the sides apart. Attach the suspension thread to the middle of these glued tabs.

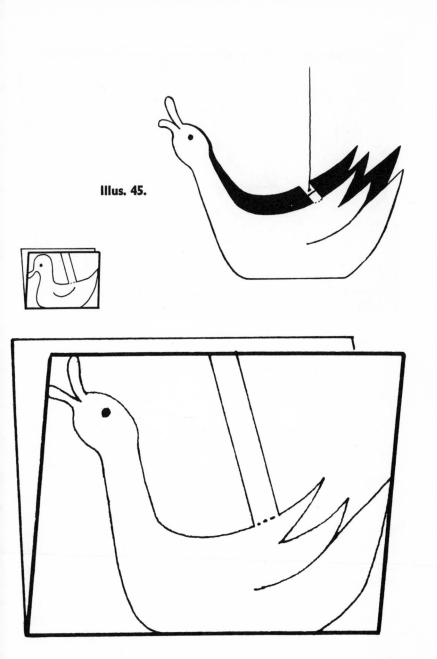

Illus. 45.

Illus. 46.

TROPICAL FISH

The ornate fish from the tropics that swim underwater in varicolored majesty can be a source of inspiration for your own fish mobiles. You will not need any elaborate skin-diving equipment to enjoy them—only a supply of glazed paper in various colors and patterns. (See Illustration 46.)

Make a few sketches of angel fish, clown fish, and similar exotic and colorful fishes in various sizes. Paste glazed marble-ized paper of assorted colors back to back (use striped paper for the clown fish) and then transfer your sketches to the varicolored paper.

Your mobile will add a gay aquatic note to wherever you hang it as your tropical fish swim majestically round and round.

WIRE FIGURES

The wire that you use to support the components of your mobiles and to make up the hanger-arms can also double in the creation of interesting wire figures. You can also use various bare (copper or aluminum) or insulated solid electrical wires. Did you know that the insulation on electrical wires comes in a variety of colors and designs?

With a few snips and twists of your pliers you can create an amusing cat or a playful mouse. Illustrations 47 to 50 show some of the figures that can be made.

Create a uniquely personal mobile by spelling the names of your friends in wire script. Suspend these from hanger-arms to make a name mobile.

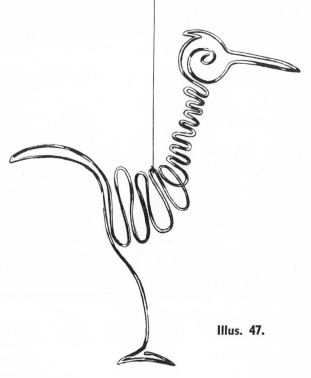

Illus. 47.

Illus. 48.

Illus. 49.

Illus. 50.

EMPTY EASTER EGGS

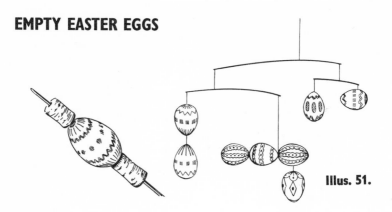

Illus. 51.

Here is a mobile that can be made the year round.

Before you can assemble this mobile, you will have to make some "empty eggs." To do this, shake some fresh eggs so that the yolks are broken and distributed with the whites. Shake well! Next, make a hole in each end of the eggs with a medium-sized needle, and suck or blow out the contents of the eggs without cracking the shells. If you prefer you can let the eggs drain into a cup by hanging them above the cup for a few hours, but for this the holes need to be larger than for blowing.

You can now apply colors or colored designs to these empty egg shells. They will last almost indefinitely. To hold the eggs while you are coloring or decorating them, thrust a long needle through the eggs and place corks on each end of the needle. You can then hold the egg by the corks while you apply your decoration.

To suspend the eggs as part of your mobile, tie a small piece of toothpick or matchstick on to a thread and carefully draw it through the hole in one end. When it gets inside the egg, the piece of wood will lie crosswise and will prevent the thread from being pulled through the opposite hole.

Arrange the eggs on the thread either in a vertical or horizontal suspension of your own design.

PLASTIC STRAW MOBILES

Plastic drinking straws—either used or unused—are the raw materials of these mobiles.

Illustration 52 shows a mobile whose flat figures are made from plastic drinking straws. (These straws are also available in glazed waxed paper, in a variety of colors, in stripes and other patterned designs.)

The trick is to join the straws by lacing through them lengthwise with colored yarn. You can construct the simple geometric figures shown on page 14, but instead of paper outline the shapes with straws.

For these you need to make your design first or to use your paper geometric mobile as a model. It is a good idea to construct an initial supporting frame of cross-members, threaded or tied with colored yarn. The resulting figure will have a rigidity yet a suppleness that will surprise you. It will delight watchers as the shapes whirl and spin in your mobile. Hang high or low, using one level or many arms.

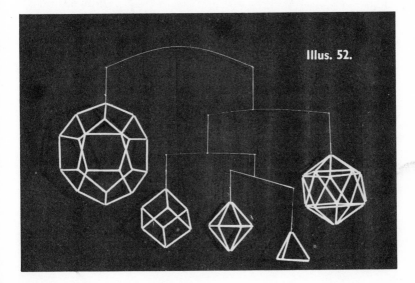

Illus. 52.

CAROUSEL

You can capture a carnival spirit with a carousel mobile.

Cut a circle of heavy glazed paper 10″ in diameter for the roof of your carousel. Just as you did with the round fish (page 44), make a cut with your knife or scissors from the edge of the circle, extending exactly to the mid-point. Now overlap one of the cut sides on to the other to form a shallow cone, and glue the edges together.

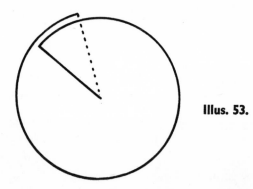

Illus. 53.

Illus. 54.

Cut a strip of paper $\frac{1}{2}''$ wide and 31" long of contrasting colored paper—a striped paper will be very effective. Cut this into a gay scalloped edge, as in Illustration 54. To complete your carousel, cut out various small animals and suspend them from the edge of the roof with fine thread.

Be sure your carousel balances when you hang it. The animals' sizes will determine how low or high you need to hang them. Experiment.

LONG FISH

For an interesting effect, combine these long fish, round fish (page 44) and flat fish (page 10)—you'll have an aquatic wonderland.

First paste sheets of colored glazed paper back to back. (They do not have to be the same color.) Cut out fish shapes as shown in Illustration 56.

Now cut an incision from the middle of the fish's body to the tail (dashed line in Illustration 56).

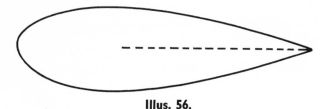

Illus. 56.

Cross the two tail parts over one another and paste them together. This will make the front part of the fish arch somewhat upwards, giving the body a three-dimensional effect.

Cut a mouth notch in the head, and paste contrasting paper eye-circles in the places indicated on the diagram.

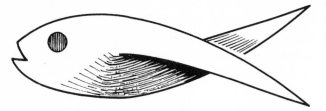

Illus. 57.

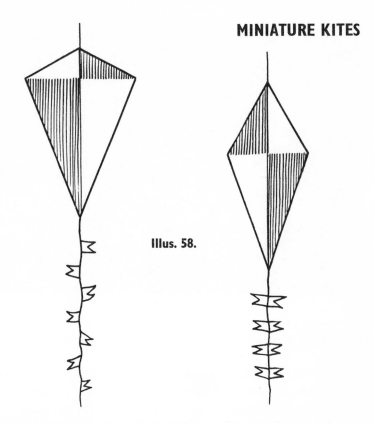

Illus. 58.

Full-size kites need a windy day to perform well; a miniature kite mobile will delight everyone in even the whisper of a wind.

Cut a variety of kite-shaped mobiles from heavy drawing paper or colored glazed paper, following Illustration 58. Fix a piece of cord to the bottom part of the kite as a tail. Glue some colorful paper streamers on this tail as shown.

You can vary the shapes of your kites by making some of them multi-sided. With the use of fine wire and tissue paper, you can even turn out some box kites that look like the real thing.

Hang them so that some float near the ceiling.

Illus. 59.

CAT AND MOUSE

Cut a flat, highly stylized cat body out of light-weight cardboard or glazed paper. (See Illustration 60.) Cut the tail separately from paper and "kink" it slightly, curling it by running it between your thumb and the cutting edge of the scissors. Or you can make the tail from Christmas gift-wrapping ribbon, curled in the same way.

Make the mice in the same fashion.   (See Illustrations 61 and 62.)

You can also make the cats and mice out of metal foil strips.

Table tennis balls can be transformed into cats (Illustration 59, right) and many different animal heads. Use hat pins with glass heads for eyes. Snip off the long ends of the pins and glue the eyes to the table tennis balls with a dab of colorless cement. Yarn or twine, shredded slightly, will provide the whiskers.

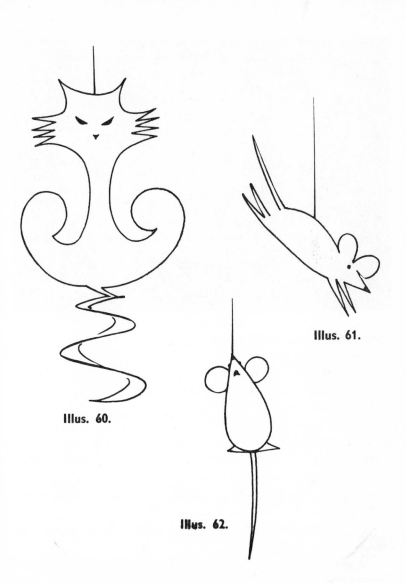

Illus. 61.

Illus. 60.

Illus. 62.

Cats are the traditional enemies of mice—but cats and mice will play together in a mobile made of these figures. Somehow the cats never can quite catch the mice!

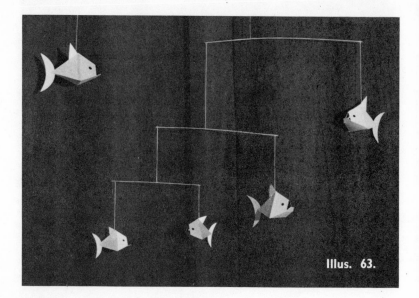

THREE-DIMENSIONAL FISH

These three-dimensional fish are an interesting change from the flat shapes you have been making.

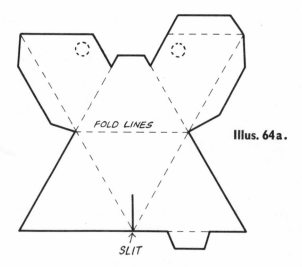

FOLD LINES

Illus. 64a.

SLIT

From flexible light-weight cardboard cut pieces to the pattern shown in Illustration 64a. The smaller triangular-shaped piece in the illustration will form the dorsal fin; the half-moon shape will make the tail. Cut these from contrasting paper or light-weight cardboard.

Fold the cardboard body along the dashed lines. Apply paste to the pasting tabs and assemble the body of the fish.

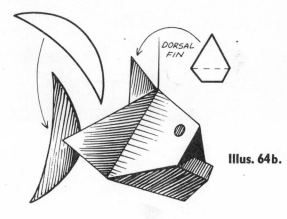

Illus. 64b.

Note that the tabs go inside.

Add the tail and the dorsal fin, applying paste to the tab on the latter.

Paste paper circles on the fish for eyes, or punch holes with a hand punch where the eyes should be.

Attach the fish to your mobile by means of a thread glued to the body at the front end of the dorsal fin.

Illustration 63 shows a whole school of these three-dimensional fish.

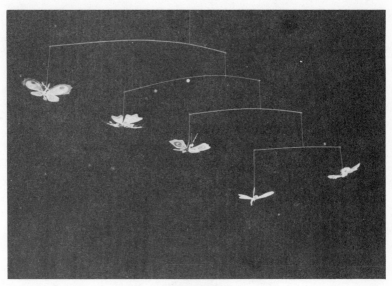

Illus. 65.

BUTTERFLIES AND DRAGONFLIES

Take a flexible piece of wire and bend it into the shape of a butterfly, as in Illustration 66. For the butterfly you need only a frame. Illustration 67 shows the outline of the dragonfly wings and body. Start and end the bending of the wire for the body at the place where the wings join it.

Now to finish the dragonfly's body, braid a short, tightly wound plait out of three strips of varicolored raffia. Tie the end of the braid with thread so that it will not unravel. Wind this around the body of the insect. Tie a knot at the front end so that two pieces of raffia (of the same color) protrude as "feelers."

Next join the wings and body together, using fine thread to tie them. Apply colorless cement to the wire wings on one side only. Affix colored rice paper or tissue paper to the wings. Leave about $\frac{1}{8}''$ edge all round. Snip this with your scissors, as you did in making the transparent fish (page 32), and paste it under the other side of the wire. Alternatively, you can leave jagged or scalloped edges protruding over the wire.

Follow the same procedure in giving your butterfly paper wings.

If you use marbleized or patterned paper for the wings, you can create a dazzling series of insects that will colorfully swoop and hover in your mobile.

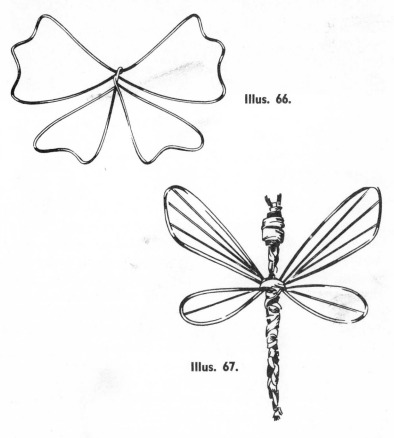

Illus. 66.

Illus. 67.

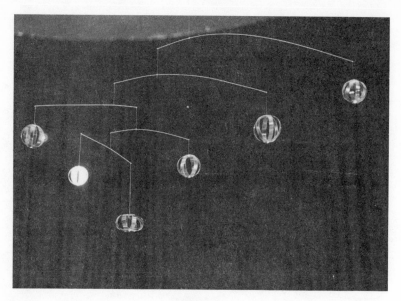

Illus. 68.

STRIPED BALLS

Here is a modern mobile that can be made with metal foil. Cut some $\frac{3}{8}$"-wide strips 8" to 12" long. For each ball you will need from 6 to 8 such strips. Take one end of each strip, hold the ends together in a circle and punch a hole through the strip ends. Now push an envelope clasp through the hole you have just punched. Bend the ends of the clasp apart to hold the strips.

Now separate the individual strips, compressing them into a ball shape. Gather the opposite (loose) ends in the same fashion as before, punch the hole and insert another envelope clasp. Spread if necessary to achieve a perfect round ball.

When you have made three or more balls, you can hang them as in the photograph.

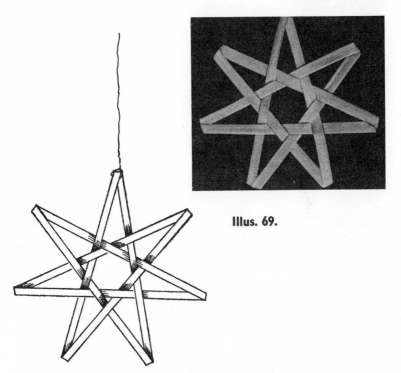

Illus. 69.

Waxed-paper straws can be flattened to provide material for making stars. Flatten the straws with the flat of a butter knife or the bowl of a spoon.

To make a seven-pointed star you will need seven flattened straws. Glue the ends of these together as shown in Illustration 69, using all-purpose glue—but first scrape the wax from the end of each straw so as to make a better joint.

Pin the straws to a board with a pin through the middle of each straw and you will find that they are easier to glue in the shape you want them. Another pin lightly through each joint will help to hold the parts being glued while the glue is drying.

SATURN'S RINGS

The rings can be of any size, but 3″ in diameter with a ring width of $\frac{3}{4}$″ will be a good proportion to use in making these or in making any enlarged rings.

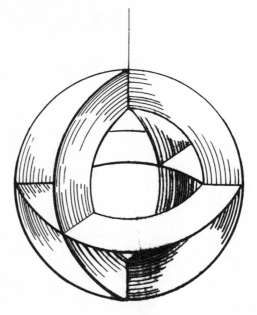

Illus. 70.

Sketch three rings on heavy colored paper as shown in Illustration 71. Notch them exactly as shown—the notches should be half the width of the ring.

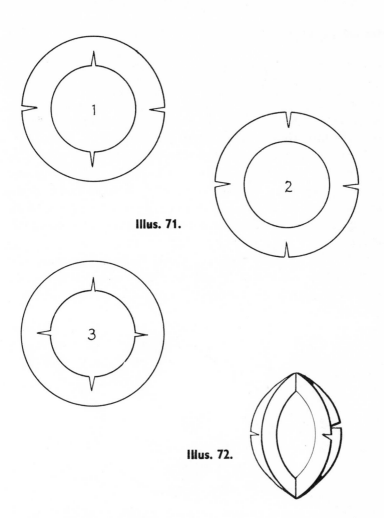

Illus. 71.

Illus. 72.

Cut out the rings and intertwine rings 1 and 2, as shown in Illustration 72. It will be a relatively simple matter to add ring 3 to the structure to complete it.

When you have acquired proficiency in making these Saturn's Rings from heavy paper, you may want to try your hand at making them from metal foil.

WIRE COMPOSITIONS

Using bare copper wire or insulated electrical bell wire and round Christmas tree ornaments, you can create interesting mobile designs that will add a touch of bright color and movement to any room. The wire hangers of the ornaments will simplify the problem of attachment.

You can create other interesting mobiles using cork balls or wooden balls (such as come with children's lawn games) or even painted table-tennis balls. Affix these by inserting the hanger arms of your mobile directly into holes drilled or punched into the balls. The different weights of the balls you use will give an interesting effect to your mobile; heavier objects tend to move about in slower fashion. Illustration 73 shows what effects can be achieved with a few simple balls and some lengths of wire.

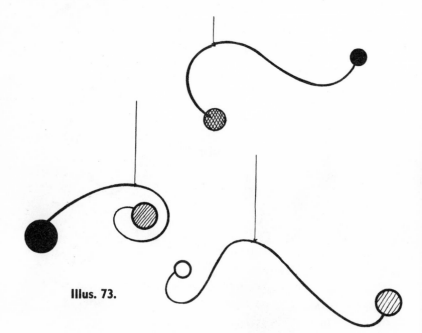

Illus. 73.

Tinkling glass chimes have been known in the Orient for centuries. This glass mobile is an adaptation of such chimes.

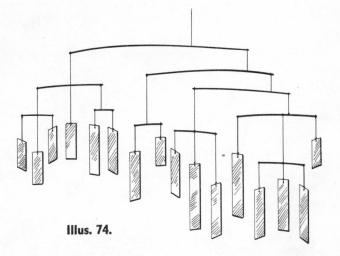

Illus. 74.

From thin glass cut strips of various lengths about 1″ wide. Varying the length of the glass strips will result in variations in the music produced by your mobile. If there is a glazier's shop near you, you can have a small hole drilled in each strip near one end. If not, fix nylon thread to each strip, using acetone-based cement.

For a more colorful effect, dye the glass strips on each side with special glass colors obtainable at your artists' supply shop.

Up until now, you have been mounting your mobiles so that the components will not touch when in motion. In this mobile, however, the objective is to arrange the glass strips so they lightly brush against one another. You may have to experiment a little to obtain the best placement for the most melodious sound. Sight and sound will then combine to make this mobile a delight to both eye and ear.

JAPANESE LANTERNS

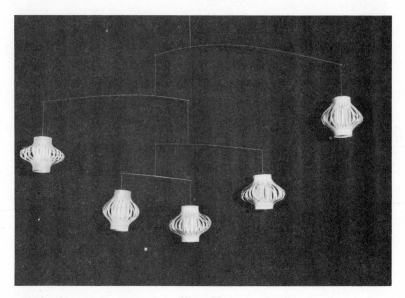

Illus. 75.

Cut a 12"-square piece of light-weight cardboard into strips (see Illustration 76). Glue the two uncut sides together with a small overlap so that a tube results. Set this tube upright on a table and press down with your hand; you will see that it is very flexible and springy.

Make another (uncut) tube of the same diameter about 8" long of light-weight cardboard and insert it inside the cut tube. Now push the top and bottom parts of the outer (cut) tube together so that it expands in an outward direction. Hold this and glue the top and bottom edges of the outside tube to the inside tube. A fine wire across the top of the lantern will serve as the hanger for attaching the suspension thread. A completed Japanese lantern mobile is featured in Illustration 75. Of course, you should not try to illuminate these "lanterns" with candles.

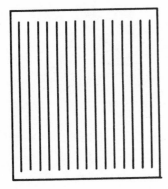

Illus. 76.

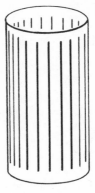

RING FISH

Illus. 77.

These imaginative, almost-abstract fish are best made from metal foil.

Cut a strip of metal foil about $\frac{1}{2}''$ in width; the length will depend upon the size fish you want to make, but 12″ will be a good average length.

Make the body of the fish from the strip of foil in this fashion: First, form the interior ring (Illustration 78), carefully glueing it with adhesive cement. Follow this with a slightly

Illus. 78.   **Illus. 79.**

larger ring which you glue directly at the spot where the first ring has been fastened (Illustration 79). Finally, coil a third ring. As you gain experience, you can start with a longer strip of metal foil and add successive rings to your fish.

Cut the fins and tail from colored paper and insert them in small cuts in the foil body of the fish. Attach them with glue.

Illus. 80.

WOOD-CHIP BIRDS

A large variety of shapes can be created from wood chips or shavings. Among the most engaging of these objects are wood-chip birds (Illustration 80). Two of these, shown on the left of the illustration, will probably be reminiscent of the ring fish (page 78); however, instead of making your wood-chip birds from a single shaving, each of the rings will be constructed separately. Glue the smallest ring first and add the successively larger ones. Then glue the head (made of rings), beak and decorative plumage to the body.

The birds on the right of Illustration 80 have been fashioned in the same way as the wire outline of the transparent fish (page 32), using wood strips instead of wire.

EMBOSSED FISH

Illus. 81.

In contrast to the ring fish (page 78), these embossed metal-foil fish will look almost lifelike.

Lay a large piece of metal foil on a thick layer of newspapers. With the aid of a sharp instrument (such as a letter opener, a nail file, a small pointed wooden dowel, or a ball point pen, the choice depending on the stiffness of the metal foil) emboss or imprint the outline, eyes, scales and fins of your fish on the foil.

Next, cut out the completed fish along the outline. Make a "mirror image" or reverse (flop-over) the design on to the other side of the fish. Next, the two parts are combined for a more realistic effect by glueing them together with model airplane cement.

Pierce the body of the fish at the balance point with a needle and fasten the suspension thread with a dab of glue.

Illustration 82 will give you an idea of what effects you can achieve with this technique. Do not be limited to making replicas of these fish, but let your imagination take over and create your own fanciful fish.

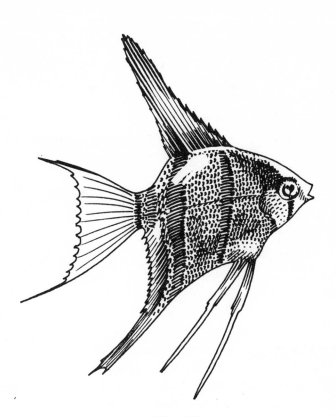

Illus. 82.

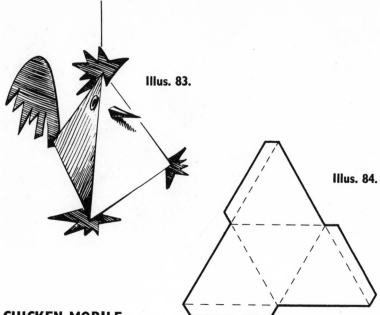

Illus. 83.

Illus. 84.

CHICKEN MOBILE

Most people need a place in the country in order to keep chickens. If space is limited, a chicken mobile is the answer.

This fanciful chicken mobile will require a rooster and several hens. The rooster can be the same shape but should be larger than the other birds. First, copy Illustration 84 on yellow light-weight cardboard. It consists of a central equilateral triangle (the sides being of equal length). This will be the base for all of your hens and roosters. Then, add to each side another equal triangle with tabs for glueing, so that there are four triangles. (The dashed lines are folding lines.)

Fold the three new triangles upwards so that they form a pyramid. Keep the sides together by glueing the tabs inside. Now cut out shapes for the tail, comb, wings, beak and eyes from red paper and glue them into the corners of the chickens' bodies. Feathers, of course, make excellent tails for them.

SHELL FISH

Illus. 85.

Nearly everyone collects shells on a vacation trip to the seashore. If you have a number of small scallop or bivalve shells you can incorporate them into a fish mobile.

For each "fish," you will need a pair of matching shells of equal size. These will be glued together but before you do so, place some colorful fluffy feathers between the shells to serve as fins and tail. (Did you know that you could tint white feathers with soluble dyes? It's easy and lots of fun!) Also, your support thread should be placed between the shells before they are glued together. Obviously, you will not be able to determine the balance point by experimentation before gluing the shells together, so try to guess it as best you can.

When the materials for your shell "sandwich" are all in place, glue the shells together, applying glue liberally around the edges and pressing them together with weights until dry.

Glue eyes on your shell fish, using discs of colored paper or metal foil. You can also use a small glass jewel or synthetic pearl as an eye, applying it to the shell with adhesive cement. A disc of colored felt punched out with your hole-puncher also makes an attractive eye.

SCALY FISH

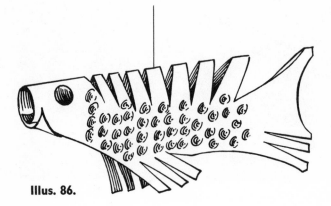

Illus. 86.

These grotesque fish are not as scary as they may seem.

Fold a long piece of flexible cardboard, and sketch on one side of it the fish shown in Illustration 87. Keeping it folded, cut out both sides of the fish at the same time.

Make scales by embossing on the outside of the fish in this way: Stand up an empty spool of thread. Rest the cardboard gently face down over the top of it, as shown in Illustration 88. With a pencil eraser press down on the cardboard where the spool hole is. After you indent the cardboard, move it a fraction of an inch and repeat the process. Do this all over the fish's body. Each time you press, you will make a small, rounded indentation in the cardboard—actually a small, scale-like bump will be embossed on the other side. Be careful to indent the cardboard just enough to raise the surface on the other side, but do not pierce it or puncture it.

Cut the eyes from glazed paper, after indenting pupils on the paper in the same way. This will give your fish's eyes a bulging, natural effect. Or you can punch out the holes for the eyes using a hand punch, but this is much less realistic.

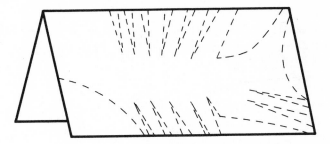

Illus. 87.

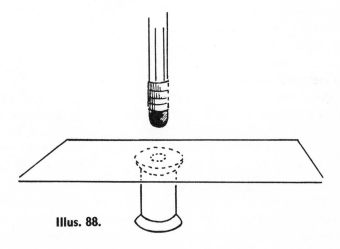

Illus. 88.

METAL COMPOSITIONS

These represent a new conception in mobiles.

Cut geometric shapes or abstract free-forms. Cut a "top" and a "bottom" for each, as shown in Illustration 89. (These do not have to be of identical size or shape.) Punch holes at the corners of each shape or in other appropriate places. Paint them on both sides in gay colors.

Now suspend the "bottom" plate from the "top" plate, using colored nylon thread. Tie knots in each thread, top and bottom, to hold them.

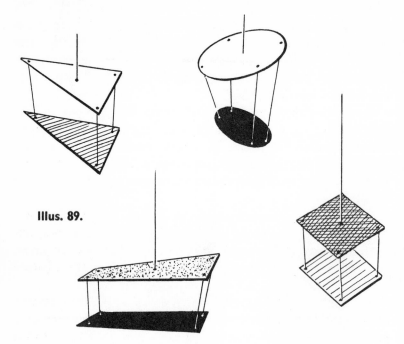

Illus. 89.

The exact balance point is not critical in suspending these compositions—as a matter of fact, many interesting effects will result if these shapes hang in somewhat lopsided fashion.

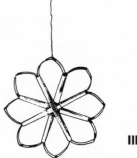

STRAW ROSETTES

Illus. 90.

Begin this design with two unflattened drinking straws of plastic or waxed paper. Cut them in half so that the pieces are about 4 inches long. Arrange the four pieces in the form of an eight-armed cross, as shown in Illustration 90 and tie them in this position with heavy thread. This will give a firm but flexible joint.

Cut eight other straws in half lengthwise. Place a dab of glue in the open ends of the straws making up the cross. Now, before the glue has a chance to dry, insert the ends of two split straws into each open straw to a depth of about $\frac{1}{2}''$. Lead the other ends into the adjacent open-ended straw piece on either side.

You can vary the design of the rosette by inserting two split halves of each straw in an open straw and skipping one open end straw before inserting the other end in an open straw. This will make each "leaf" of the rosette overlap the adjacent rosette "leaf."

For still another variation, which is actually a combination of both rosettes, make a rosette as described in the preceding paragraph and insert *four* split straws into each open-ended straw. Two of the split straws should be long and two should be short. Lead the short straw into the adjacent open-ended straw and glue. Lead the longer straw into the next open-ended straw. Do this all the way round for an interesting effect.

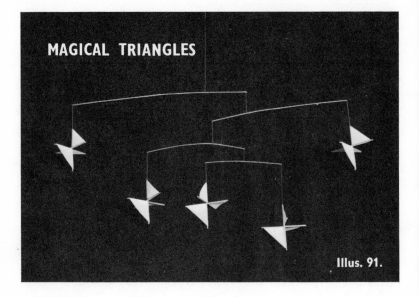

MAGICAL TRIANGLES

Illus. 91.

For each of these you will need three right-angle isosceles triangles cut from light-weight cardboard, some plastic drinking straws and three thin wooden dowels. Cut squares of cardboard in half diagonally to get triangles of the proper shape. Snip off a tiny corner of each triangle at the apex only.

Now paste pieces of plastic drinking straws to the two legs of each triangle (i.e., not the base of the triangle) and snip off the excess of the straws so that they are the same length as the legs of the triangles (Illustration 92). Slide thin wooden dowels through the straws of one triangle (dowels 1/16″ in diameter will be about right). Coat the dowels with glue before inserting them in the straws.

Next slide a second triangle over the exposed part of the dowel glued to the first triangle's straw. Glue the second triangle to the dowel by coating the dowel with glue.

Repeat this procedure with the third dowel, slipping it through the empty straw of the second triangle. Then glue the straw of the third triangle to the third dowel (Illustration

93). Cut the dowels off so that they are almost flush with the ends of the straws.

Suspend your completed magical triangles by attaching thread to one of the dowel ends and watch them whirl round merrily with every breeze (Illustration 91).

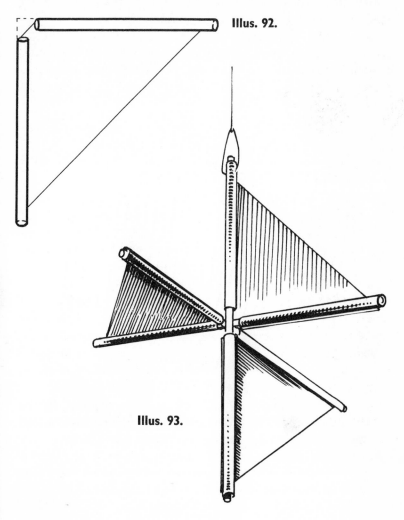

Illus. 92.

Illus. 93.

FISH TRAPS

Mix these "fish traps" with your fish mobiles for a mobile that will be an interesting conversation piece.

Cut a strip of paper 7¼" wide and 6" in length and fold it lengthwise down the middle. (See Illustration 94.) Now make a number of equidistant cuts every ¼", starting these at the fold. Cut them straight but stop within ¼" from the edges of the

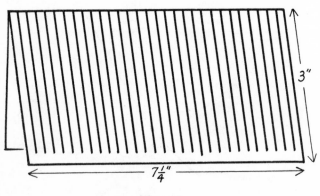

Illus. 94.

folded paper. (NOTE: No matter what dimensions you use, there should be an odd number of strips after you have made these parallel cuts.)

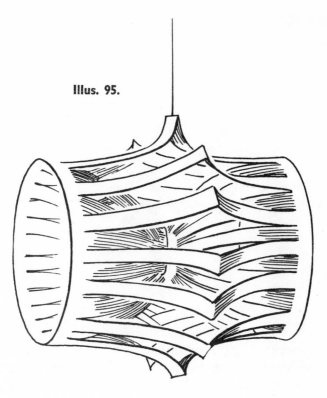

Illus. 95.

Next unfold and flatten the paper on the table. Fold every other strip in the opposite direction. Tie a piece of thread around the strips that are inside the "fish trap" to hold them tight. Use the free end of the thread to suspend your mobile.

Glue the two ends together. (These will have to be outward-pointing folds.) If you wish, this mobile can be suspended vertically as well as horizontally.

METAL FOIL STARS

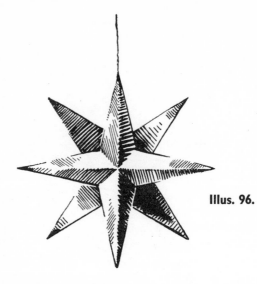

Illus. 96.

Stars can be made from metal foil or from gold- or silver-covered paper. If gold- or silver-covered paper is used, make sure that the glue you are using does not loosen the gold or silver foil from the paper. Test a small piece, and change glues if necessary.

There are certain basic folds that will be used in the projects that follow:

Triangular fold: Starting with a square, fold one corner over to meet the diagonally opposite corner. Open the paper. Repeating the triangular fold with the remaining two corners will result in a "cross" joining the corners of the square.

Book fold: Cover one half of a square with the other half so that a rectangle is formed. The result is called a "book." Open the book and fold the square in the opposite direction. A cross will now join the sides of the square.

Make the stars shown in Illustration 96 from metal foil or gold and silver paper. Such stars will make excellent components for a mobile (make the stars in assorted sizes for a more effective composition). Hang them on your Christmas tree as ornaments, or hang a large star in your window or on your door as a holiday decoration.

For each star cut two identical squares of material (metal foil, gold or silver paper, etc.) The size of your square will determine the height of the finished star you make.

Fold two triangular folds and two book folds in each square. The result will look like Illustration 97. Cut in at the middle of the four sides of each square along solid lines "a-b," as shown in the illustration. Make this cut about $\frac{1}{5}$ of the length of a side of the square. If the square measures 5″ on a side, make the cut 1″ deep. A 10″ square should be cut in 2″.

Fold each side marked "c" in Illustration 97 in toward the diagonals "d." Overlap and glue each of the "c" flaps, so that the star has a three-dimensional effect. Make a second star in exactly the same fashion and fasten the stars back to back so that they look like Illustration 96.

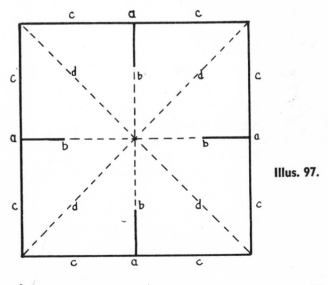

Illus. 97.

FOUR-POINTED STAR

For this star, use double-sided metal foil paper. First fold a square of this paper into a triangular fold (page 92). Open it and make a book fold (page 92). Now open the square once again; it will look like Illustration 97.

Make three folds parallel to one side of the square, creasing these alternately downwards and upwards. Each of these creases parallel to the sides of the square will go only as far as the diagonal creases joining the opposite corners. Repeat this along each of the remaining three sides. The result will be a series of three concentric square strips surrounding a central square. (See Illustration 99).

Fold down the outside strip all round. (Imagine that this square of metal foil paper is a large table cloth set over a smaller table so that the edges and corners hang down all around.) Indent the next inner crease downwards so that the outer fold is like a "fence" all around the raised inner square.

Using both hands take hold of each of two diagonally opposite ends with your thumb and middle finger, and with your index finger press *down* on the portion of the diagonal fold enclosed between them. With your ring finger or little finger, press *up* on the next inner portion of the diagonal fold —the one closest to the central square. Repeat this with the remaining two opposite corners, flexing each set of corners until the star assumes the desired shape (Illustration 98.) Depress the central square slightly.

You will now have a star with four points; besides its usefulness in mobiles, this star can serve as a Christmas tree decoration or—used on a table—as an appealing candle holder.

Illus. 98.

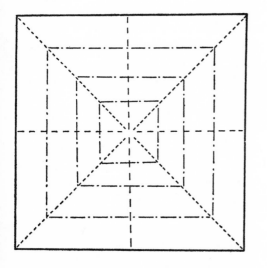

Illus. 99.

INDEX